SEVEN STEPS SWITCHES TO EXCELLENCIES

Firm and Exquisite in Manifestation

SEVEN STEPS SWITCHES TO EXCELLENCIES

MIND DIET, UNLEASH YOUR DESIRES

OLOU-FEMY SATTY

Xulon Press
2301 Lucien Way #415
Maitland, FL 32751
407.339.4217
www.xulonpress.com

© 2023 by Olou-Femy Satty

All rights reserved solely by the author. The author guarantees all contents are original and do not infringe upon the legal rights of any other person or work. No part of this book may be reproduced in any form without the permission of the author.

Due to the changing nature of the Internet, if there are any web addresses, links, or URLs included in this manuscript, these may have been altered and may no longer be accessible. The views and opinions shared in this book belong solely to the author and do not necessarily reflect those of the publisher. The publisher therefore disclaims responsibility for the views or opinions expressed within the work.

Unless otherwise indicated, Scripture quotations taken from the King James Version (KJV) – *public domain*.

Paperback ISBN-13: 978-1-66286-504-6
Hard Cover ISBN-13: 978-1-66286-505-3
Ebook ISBN-13: 978-1-66286-506-0

Special Thanks

Jennifer Miller- Graphic Designer

Rachel Arterberry- Editor and Foreword By

Rosemary Aboh- E-book graphic

Preet Kamal- Cover design inspiration
Christopher Baten - Book- Website and Logo

Kelly Bright

Gilman J. Michaud

Pastor Kalinsky, Great woman of God

My daughter Lovely Jourdan

Special Thanks to all my friends and family for the inspiration

To God be the glory
Hebrews 11: 1
Habakkuk 2: 3-4
Isaiah 58: 12

Firm and Exquisite in Manifestation

TABLE OF CONTENTS

Foreward...ix
Introduction xi

SEVEN SWITCHES

Switch 1: Cleansing Your Words!..........................1
Switch 2: Have A Date With Yourself..................... 5
Switch 3: Discover or Find Your Desire(s).................. 9
Switch 4: Meditation!................................... 11
Switch 5: Faith - See Yourself Accomplishing Your Desires.... 13
Switch 6: Be Responsible 19
Switch 7: Serenity!..................................... 21
Conclusion.. 25

Firm and Exquisite in Manifestation

Foreword

As a Christian, the title and theory of this book drew me in. I believe, as does the author, that we are all born of noble birth. Our light can be dimmed or made brighter by our actions during our lifetime, and with practice and developing habits that coincide with God's word can help us achieve all that we desire.

A Mind Diet as I see it is a system or method of guiding each of us to follow in Jesus' footsteps to ensure not only eternal life but to help us walk in the path that God has predestined for us, bringing about peace, joy, and happiness during our time here on earth.

Allow Seven Steps Switches to Excellencies to be your guide to unleashing your desires, taking charge of your life, and leading others as God intended. I hope you will enjoy discovering how you can turn on each switch in your life, reap the rewards, and achieve the abundance the Lord, Our Savior, has promised.

Be Blessed!
Rachel Arterberry
Author

Firm and Exquisite in Manifestation

Introduction

Excellencies are life maintenance services. It is the concept and ideology that we all as individuals are noble by creation. We are children of God. We are children of The infinite God. We are endowed with great abilities and through a good use of our mind, live nobly. Nobleness is not a trait or character quality set aside for certain well-defined people of honor but is given and available at the reach of all (poor or rich, young or old, developed or third-world country, Christian or not). It is all in how an individual sees life or is brought up to see life. It is a mindset. A life of excellence, nobleness of character, a God-like way of thinking, and living in harmony with oneself and their environment depends on a few simple habits. These habits that we call "switches" are easy to do and easy not to. We are already doing them in some ways in our daily lives; our goal is to bring more awareness of how we go about daily life to get a positive life experience. Excellencies is a "Mind Diet." When you see any man or woman who has succeeded in any endeavor, you see a person with a good mind diet. A good mind diet opens the door to discovering one's divine desire, which is, in fact, one's direction in life. A man/woman without desire is a person with no direction in life. It is like a ship in the harbor with no destination; it never leaves the port, and even if it does for one reason or another, it goes wherever the wind blows. That is not a way to live this precious life that has been given to us at a great price.

We create our own life, believe it or not, through our habits and make it better through these switches, which are also dimmable:

1- Switch 1: Cleansings

2- Switch 2: Date with self

3- Switch 3: Discover what one wants in life.

4- Switch 4: Meditation

5- Switch 5: Faith, see yourself accomplish your desires.

6- Switch 6: Take charge of your life; be responsible.

7- Switch 7: Serenity

SWITCH 1
CLEANSING YOUR WORDS!

Dictionaries define cleansing as to make clean. It is to be removed by cleaning. To clean has a few good definitions, but staying right on point to our objective, tidying up, or getting rid of undesirable persons or features seems suitable. Cleaning our words by weeding out all the negative is particularly important for any desire we intend to achieve. The conversations we have, the speeches we make daily bring us closer to the healthy and wealthy desirable life we all want or take us far from it. You can't want a strong, fit, healthy body, and, at the same time, we all talk and converse about sicknesses or continue conversations about folks we know or read about with this and that kind of disease.

Our words have power. The Bible told us this through various scriptures in different ways to get our attention on the matter, but we humans don't seem to take that seriously. Why? Is it by ignorance, lack of understanding of the scriptures, or simple lack of faith? John 10:34 and Psalms 82:6 say that "Ye are gods." Isaiah 55:11 says, "So shall my word be that goeth forth out of my mouth: it shall not return unto me void, but shall accomplish that which I please, and it shall prosper in the thing whereto I sent it." Humans are like God, created in His image; Anything man/woman speaks or comes out of her/his mouth will not come back void. It will manifest or create exactly what you said. You talk about, for example, the fact that people do not like you;

ultimately, they will not like you. But if you talk about being likable, you will have pleasing and likable folks around you. This is more common among humans talking about lack and not having enough money or time; you will not have enough of any of those.

This is the biggest of all, the use of "I AM." In the book of Exodus, when Moses asked God His name, according to the story, God told Moses to tell the children of Israel that I AM sent me. I AM is God's name. What is so interesting to see throughout the centuries is that the "I AM" is a very important part or the most important part of any language ever spoken on earth to describe one's state of being. Any person in any language uses I Am to point to himself (name) or situations they are in. It is shown throughout the Bible how the I AM is loving, kind, abundant, powerful, and all kinds of good adjectives to describe Him. You barely (never) hear I AM followed by any negative words except when man uses it 99% of the time. I AM is supposed to be the name of God. The Bible also said that God would not make guiltless those who use His name in vain. We wonder why our world is so negative, and we want positive but still confess and talk negatively all the time. The Bible even said, "let the weak say, I am strong."

This first switch is very important for men or women who want a positive and healthy life full of joy, happiness, wealth, and love. In our daily life, speak good and positive words. Clean as much as possible of your conversation. (Guide it to the goal you intend to achieve in life.) Say, 'I can' more often. Use positive words to describe yourself as much as possible even though your current "reality" shows differently. We are not saying that nothing negative will ever happen. That is up to you and how big your goal is in life. The bigger your goals, the greater should be your positivity. For this purpose, we just want you to be 51 - 55%. It is like a battery in your car. If the arrow on your dashboard is over 50%, that battery is good. For you, too, keeping your words (conversations) over 51% means you are on the right track leading to a happy, healthy, and wealthy life. This percentage increases as your positive habits grow; one of the reasons why this switch 1 and all others to come are dimmable from 1 to 10. One (1) is your lowest negativity, and then ten (10) is the highest positivity. It depends on the day. Your conversation might be more positive today than another day or more negative. It is all in what reality you brought to your experience that day. The negative is like the weeds in the garden; they will always grow no matter how many occasions you kill or weed them out to serve a purpose. They give the ground some protection and vegetation and, in some way, help the crops grow. Weeds give the world contrast for growth and stability and eco-balance. You must have the negative to a certain extent depending on what you are creating, but you cannot afford more negative than positive in the same substance. It will not work; thet project will fail; so will your life when you have more negative than positive. To be fine means staying and continuing on that positive track in your daily conversations is where switch 2 comes in as an establishment.

Firm and Exquisite in Manifestation

Notes

SWITCH 2
HAVE A DATE WITH YOURSELF

You have learned the importance of staying positive (cleansing). You have done switch 1 for at least seven days. We recommend twenty-one days for those who have never heard of positive conversations.

When you do it for a while, you will see improvement in your mental state. Life will start appearing to be different in a better way than you are used to. People are nicer to you. You have more energy to start and finish your days. Now it is time to schedule a date with yourself.

Dictionaries define a date as a social appointment or engagement arranged beforehand with another person, especially when a romantic relationship exists or may develop. Here they have a date with another person, but you will be alone by yourself in this case of our lecture or ideology. Find a quiet place you love and like to go to. Try to make this as natural as possible without strain or anxiety, and dressing up is unnecessary. I know that a first date can be full of anxiety, excitement, and mixed emotions in a relationship. But this one makes it like you are just going for a walk somewhere quiet. It can be in the comfort of your own home, but we suggest outdoors, in nature will give you a better result. You can see birds, trees and maybe other people depending on what location you choose. The less crowded is better and try to be alone with no disturbances, cell phone turned on silent or Do Not Disturb mode. Our goal here is to enjoy quiet time to appreciate yourself, your life, the beauty of nature. We want you to find things you love about yourself (your body, work, situations). PLEASE do not compare yourself or your life with another person. We just want you to love you for who you are and enjoy the moment of gratefulness. If any negative thoughts about you come up, put them aside and just appreciate and love yourself. Nobody will love you if you do not first love yourself. Nobody will appreciate, congratulate, promote, cheer, etc.... all the good things you want and desire unless you start to want it and do it with yourself.

You see, our daily conversations are more positive when we appreciate and love ourselves NO MATTER what circumstance we are in. We might be broke, have no home, no friends, it does not matter. We always feel alive and excited when we learn to appreciate ourselves. This should be done at least once weekly for the first ninety days of the process. We must make sure we are consistent with it weekly. And here, the keyword is "consistent"; this is the only way to ensure positive progress in what we are working toward. In the first couple weeks, you might have to use a little discipline in committing to it, but after that, as you are feeling better, it becomes natural to find a quiet time, even if it is as little as five minutes to get you into that gratitude moment. We must remember to continue practicing switch 1; in fact, we must make this a lifestyle: practice Self-Love or Love-Self.

PS: No great men/women (gurus, prophets, leaders) ever becomes great without mastering this switch 2. I suggest that you do your own research on this, you will be surprise how high they all value it in their own ways. Even Jesus Christ, the Lord of the Lords always takes times for himself, especially after miracles. Do you know why? Because He knew the power of it. He knew that all those men kind weaknesses (sicknesses, diseases, emotional issues) that men call reality are not God's true reality for men. Men's fallen to acquainted with his identity of Sons and Daughters of God is the cause of all those diseases. Jesus Christ ministry was and is to reestablish men kind to that original state. He accomplished it beautifully showing men how to do it then and dwelling in all men today. So he took times for himself after all those miracles to cleanse himself from those diseases and emotional issues to realign himself with the true reality of God and recharge himself.

As you see a Date with one's self has to be part of our routine. So, having done switch 1 and adding switch 2 for a while, it is time to start looking forward to the next switch.

Firm and Exquisite in Manifestation

Notes

_____
_____
_____
_____
_____
_____
_____
_____
_____
_____
_____
_____

SWITCH 3
DISCOVER OR FIND YOUR DESIRE(S)

The gardener has a nice seed that he planted in his wonderful garden. A couple of weeks went by, and life happened, an emergency call here and there, a planned road trip, kids going to after-school activities. You cannot miss church and all activities of the evening: we must be a good Christian and have fellowship, right? All these are great and wonderful reasons and have a valuable point. But at the same time, the weeds overtook the garden. You wonder why your nice seed is not growing even though it is a highly efficient seed. Annoyed by the whole situation, you decide one day to pull out all the weeds and do some cleanup. Like good fortune, the rain comes; it is amazing how good fortune shows up at the right time. Suddenly, something pops out of the ground, and it is your seed that started growing. This is what happens with our desires.

The seed is our desire(s). It is what the Creator has put inside of us from birth. We all have a least one. The Bible says that He gave us a measure of faith, which we will go into more detail in switch 5. But for now, just know that you are born with some desire that you are to bring forth in measure to live a beautiful, fulfilling God-like life on this earth, contrary to what some might make you believe that a poor life and suffering is the will of God to get you to Heaven. I will boldly say it is a lie that goes against the nature of God.

In this switch, you will discover what you really want in life. Let us say that this is not a time to figure out how the desires will come about. You just go ahead and write down all that you want in life, what excites you. This process would come easily if you did switch 1 and 2 right and continue to do it. Bringing back the gardening analogy again, switches 1 and 2 weed out the garden and get it ready for the seed, which is your desire. You have made the ground ready for the last few weeks with all the cleansing and your alone time. One thing to know here is that our desires will never end. There will always be more and more to come as long as your soul liveth. Some things you desire today may not be what you want tomorrow. Just find what you want today.

The next thing is asking yourself why you want them. Everything we want in our experience ultimately is for the feeling of it; from material possessions to relationships, the result is about the feeling of emotion. We can name a few of them here: happiness, joy, fulfillment, accomplishment, being wanted, pride, aliveness, and the list goes on and on.

After that, go back to each desire and do the best you can to describe the specific emotion attached to that desire. This is very important in fulfilling your desire—it is something that we will discuss in detail in switch 5 on Faith.

Word of warning: throughout this process, you can desire anything you want in life, good or bad. There is no exception if you follow and do these steps correctly. Remember, there is a law that governs this Universe put in place by the Creator that I call God; I do not care how you call Him. It doesn't matter to me. You reap what you sow. If you use this to sow evil, you will get the result of it. You might get away with it for a while, but it will catch up to you over time. Here in the platform of Excellencies, we promote wellness, well-being, the fruits of the spirit like mentioned in the book of Philippians 4:8 for life in abundance and God-like way of life, which will be elaborated on more in the next switch.

SWITCH 4
MEDITATION!

The dictionary defines meditation as spiritual introspection, which is the act of looking within oneself. It is a mental process that you practice calming yourself to be at ease. In the process of meditation, one learns to extract himself from their present situations, circumstances, and what we so-call reality and fixes their mind on nothingness. The objective is to get the "practitioner" to clear their mind of all negativities.

To use this analogy, it is like to reboot oneself to the manufacturer's state, which is original and put in receiving mode after your mind is all cleared out of negativities to hear from God, the Universe, Source, or whatever you call the Creator. I said it before, and it is worth repeating. I do not care how you call The Creator.

Some might call this prayer session which I can partially agree with, but it is more than that. My response here comes from years of experience and growth in Christian organizations. Most of the time, we go to God in prayer, talking for most of the time we are in the session and not letting God talk to us a bit. It might be a little acceptable if our talk is positive. It is not usually. All we have learned to say to God is our unworthiness, how bad we feel, and how our circumstances are disastrous. We spend that time ordering God to change the situation out of fear, and ultimately, we come out even worse than the way we were before we got in. We are wondering why we have not changed even though we pray to God all the time. This is not a knock on Christianity or any Christian organization per se.

I have done it myself for years and get a glimpse occasionally of prayer answers, but it could be better. Some critics may say it's just you. I have prayed that way and have gotten multiple prayers answered. Wonderful for you, God Bless. Imagine what it could be if you pray right, one hundred-fold more: Your God is a God of abundance. In fact, I have known and know some spiritual leaders, pastors who even condemn that way of prayer from their followers and even taught them how to use fewer words in prayer and let God talk to them. I am under one of those leaders now who pastors the church beautifully. She does her best to correct other believers from that way of praying.

Our life (every second, minute, hour, and day) should be in prayer. Prayer is to be in tune with God, meaning that you and God are one; Christ in you and you in Him. So, everything I do and every word I speak must be God-like. I will go into more detail about this in switch 6. Then when I take time alone for what I call meditation, you can call it prayer, it is to calm myself in His presence to be recharged to continue my life journey. And even then, if I have something to say, it should be words of praise and thanksgiving. We should not even use that moment for many of those; I will say 1/10 of that time is my suggestion. We should be thankful and grateful all day long in all our affairs. This same principle applies when we gather as a congregation. Enter His house with praise and thanksgiving, the Bible says.

Meditation, in my opinion, should be done at least twice a day, the first thing the morning when you wake and right before bed. I will add that one can try their best to find time during the day for a few minutes to practice it. It is important for our body, mind, and soul to direct us to our purpose in life.

SWITCH 5
FAITH - SEE YOURSELF ACCOMPLISHING YOUR DESIRES

In my life observations and experience, I have seen many negative and positive accomplishments, all having one essential common denominator, "Faith." I did not think of it or see it until a few days ago in my search for a summary chapter to this marvelous book. It dawned on me that every single attribute and quality that anybody that ever succeeded in his chosen field has underneath one seed and only one seed called faith.

You must have faith to start, do whatever is needed, and have faith to get up and continue after facing some failures. Discipline, persistence, willpower, resistance, to name a few, have to do with belief. Paul J. Meyer said, "There's magic in believing." Faith gives us miracles; it helps us surmount any adversity or temporary defeat. The Bible says, "With faith, all things are possible." So, what is faith? Why is it essential in our development?

First, let us check the definition starting with the Bible. I love the Bible and believe it is the greatest book ever written and the words of God.

The Bible indeed is the words of God (as Universal Mind, All-Knowing All-Wise, All Perfect, All Love...) plus positive manifestations of words of God when applied positively, plus the negative manifestations of that same word of God when applied negatively. It is two edges of a sword depending on the mind who uses it. And we see that throughout the Bible, it is put together for our instructions and guidance on living our lives God-like.

The Bible says in Hebrews 11:1, *"Now faith is the substance of the things hoped for, the evidence of things not seen."*

Faith is a substance of goals, dreams, or objects we want or want to accomplish.

Now, what is substance? I like this definition: The actual matter of a thing, as opposed to the appearance or shadow; It is the reality.

The Bible continues to say, the evidence of things not seen. And the evidence means plain or clear to the sight or understanding.

Now let us look at that verse again, taking into consideration the definition of the words: Hebrews 11:1, *"Now faith is the actual matter of thing as opposed to the appearance or shadow; faith is the reality of things hoped for; the plain or clear to the sight (mental perception or regard) or understanding of things not seen."*

You must have a clear mental picture(s) of desires and see yourself with it or doing it.

Faith can be made perfect by applications.

This definition of faith is enough for me to prove my point. Any other definitions of faith you might find all derived from the Bible in one way or another.

Everyone has needs and wants. We have goals and aspirations that might be equal to our purpose or different from what we want to see realized. The only ingredient that guarantees the fulfillment of those desires and aspirations is faith. I strongly advise that you read that definition repeatedly and apply it to whatever that objective is for you. The Bible never lies; God never lies. He created all things by faith through His Words. I would suggest that you dig more into the Bible because it is a road map for true success that respects and involves humanity.

This is my belief that there is no such thing as success that does not benefit humanity.

FAITH IS VISUALIZATION OR IMAGINATION.

So often, we separate these three as if they are different from each other.

Visualization is a mental image of things desired; it is to picture them as already in possession. It is seeing yourself mentally already doing that which you want to do or want to have.

Imagination is a conception or mental creation of what is not actually present to the senses as is.

We already went through the definition of **faith** in the first paragraph. You cannot help seeing the similitude of these three words. Christians often call people that use visualization and imagination spiritualists or engaging in ungodly practices. But the word faith is welcome in Christian's vocabulary, which brings me to question if Christians really understand what faith is. Seeing Christian lives full of diseases, poverty, unhappiness, and covetousness is proof that the word faith is somehow misused. God's people are supposed to be the most prosperous and healthy people on earth, but we are seeing the opposite. We use the excuse of Jesus Christ's return and life after death in Heaven as justification. Christians should learn how to use and practice faith more than preach it. Practice faith, then preaching faith, and the Kingdom of God will take care of itself. We do not have to convince anybody about God and Who He is. They will see it in Christians through love, joy, prosperity, peace, health, and all-in abundance.

We see God as a prosperous God throughout the Bible, but on earth, we see His servants or children extremely poor and unhappy hoping to die and go to Heaven for a better life. Why?

The wealthy people are the people Christians call at times, people of the world they preach against. But the paradox is that the same Christians go to so-called children of the world for jobs and money when they need it. I believe it is a time for a paradigm shift among my fellow Christians. We must learn how to use faith properly to get the blessings of God.

God has established His blessings as a law of buoyancy that follows certain principles. Whosoever does it will get the blessings. It does not matter if the person is righteous or not. The Bible said He sends His rain on just and unjust. Whoever catches the rain (or builds a reservoir to catch the rain) will get water, a good man or bad man. But He did say that the bad man will pay for his evil-doing, and His mercy covers us all.

The question will be for a Christian, what is the benefit of serving God then? The first is Heaven, of course, and second, if you build the reservoir to catch the rain, He will protect, give you peace and joy over it and make sure it lasts. What about that for blessings?

Christians must learn how to visualize or imagine; it is faith. But before then, Christians and all of us must discover what we want to accomplish or achieve in this world. That is what this little book can help you do. We are not put here by accident to live and suffer and die to go to Heaven. Secondly, Christians must stop preaching against and condemning the world. Whatever you sow, so shall you reap.

I don't like to get into discussions, but one day, for some reason, I got into a discussion about faith with this gentleman, and he was quoting the scripture that reads: "Faith cometh by hearing the word of God." He continued to tell of all the prophecies of things to come as if I am new to the Bible. It is sad to see that with all the goodness of the Bible, the man focused on the small negative parts and found justification for those parts that power and feed our fears and laziness. It is not okay to sit and to do nothing and hope for God to come live our life for us.

In this life, we must work, not even too much hard labor but work hard to understand God's principle of creation and let those laws work for us, not against us. It is working now and, for the most part, against my fellow Christians, and we need to wake up. Except for a few that know it and use it well, it gives them all that God promised on this earth, but they are afraid to say how they obtained it out of fear of being labeled a spiritualist. Some that do have been labeled for sure by so-called Christians.

How to Use Faith Effectively

It does not matter what you call it; faith, visualization, or imagination. Just practice the definitions of faith at the top of this chapter. Use it for anything you want and see God do a miracle in your life. Remember, if you abuse it and use it for evil, it will produce evil in your life, and there is always a consequence for evil or anything we manifest. Bring to creation good things for humanity, and your blessings will overflow.

We must be fully positive and focus on what we want and not deny it by our actions and words at the same time. We must do so effortlessly by visualization and not forcing anything into existence. By forcing, we show a lack of faith in giving power to anything other than God, the Only Creator.

For example, you cannot pray and believe for healing and at the same time be thinking or talking to folks about how bad your sickness or how incurable that is. That is not faith.

Another example is believing for wealth and money and talking about lack and not having enough or how hard things are or how you can't afford this or that.

Firm and Exquisite in Manifestation

Notes

SWITCH 6
BE RESPONSIBLE

To accomplish anything in life, there must be personal responsibility at all levels. It is even more important when one has a definite goal or goals to achieve. Talking about achieving, we realize that nothing is ever created in this world without being first thought about. Everything from a toothbrush to the most sophisticated machines ever built in this generation was first started in the mind of someone as a thought. The mind is like a garden and is the starting place (beginning) of all creations. That being said, if we want to achieve anything in this life for ourselves, it has to come first through our mind, the thoughts that we think in every moment.

Again, using the analogy of the mind as a garden. If I want to grow tomatoes in my garden, the first thing I must do is get my garden ready for the tomato plants: get the ground cultivated, weeded out, filled with proper soil, and watered ready for the plants. This calls for personal responsibility for the tasks at hand. When the tomatoes are planted, it takes even more responsibility to take care of them until they reach a point of surviving the natural elements by themselves and give them objective desires. Everybody understands this botanical aspect but gets confused when it comes to the mind. Believe it or not, it is the same principle that operates in relation to the mind. We must take responsibility for our minds and the thoughts that come through them.

We must do our best to discover that treasure and use it effectively. "The mind is the greatest but unexplored Continent of our life," to quote Earl Nightingale. We must make it our major task to discover the operation of our mind and sow good thoughts into it. Those thoughts create our life. Good, positive, and divine thoughts give a great and wonderful life. Negative, unworthy thoughts give us a life of failure and misery we surely do not desire.

The Bible said, "As a man thinketh of his heart, so he is." Philosophers over the centuries have declared that our thoughts are things. So, what you think is what you believe, and it is what you become.

Take responsibility for controlling your thoughts and directing them towards the objective desires and weed out all negativity in your mind that deprives you of achieving it.

Think of good and positive thoughts; talk and confess always good and positive words or affirmations; feel good and have positive feelings about yourself and others. I just introduced you to three things (elements) responsible for ninety percent of a successful life, full of joy, love, health, wealth, or any goods you desire. Take charge and direct them well, and they, in return, will serve you well. They build your reality. FEM responsibility.

SWITCH 7
SERENITY!

Serenity is the last switch, for it is, "The last lesson of culture, the fruitage of the soul. It is precious as wisdom, more desired than gold—yea, than even fine gold," as James Alain mentioned in his book "As a Man Thinketh." Any man who is serene is the man who has achieved. He is the man or woman who is finished. He is poised; nothing disturbs him. He knows what he knows, and he is greatly confident.

"Calmness of mind...," that which we call serenity "... is one of the beautiful jewels of wisdom. It is the result of long patient effort in self-control; its presence is an indication of ripened experience and more than ordinary knowledge of the laws and operations of thought." James Allen again. The person who achieved serenity is the person who has overcome life's outer circumstances and focuses on the inner. He knows the laws and how things around him have come to existence, so he is no longer influenced by those situations or circumstances but is calm and always poised. He knows that all in his life experience results from thoughts that he has sent forward. He knows that if there is any situation in his life that he does not want, he just needs to change his thought and wait patiently for change. He has come to understand that worries, frets, anxieties, and fears only make the matter worse: whatever energy you send out always comes back to you. So, he does his due diligence to keep himself out of those negative energies but focuses firmly and exquisitely on the objective end of his goals.

We call this our last switch, FEM (F.E.M. = Firmly and Exquisitely Manifesting) or achievement because it is the quality in man's character that allows him to sustain success in an ideal pursuit. I have never seen anybody achieve his ideal goal and sustain that for a long time without such quality. Oh yes, you can have any success in this world with an explosive, bad temper with no respect for anyone whatsoever. You can have wealth consciousness with a bad temper but name one who sustains it. Either he lost it all, or on his way down, he turned it around and focused on that virtue which we call serenity.

Serenity is knowing that all is well. It is knowing that you are Gods and that you have the power over any adversity, situation, circumstance, and even elements. Nothing has power over your divine paths, which has been already set for you but you, yourselves. So, situations good or bad are there on the paths either as a springboard or to strengthen you in your way of attainment. A serene man/woman is thankful and grateful for all. He/she sees good in all. What a powerful and exciting way to live! In his/her doing so, he/she sees an increase in wealth, success, and prosperity. Wow!

So, we want to help you find your divine desires, achieve them, and put you on the divine path to infinite health, wealth, and success where all are done for you in divine order.

This chapter of serenity cannot be complete without mentioning the greatest human ever to live over two thousand years ago. He was and is the master of all masters of serenity: Jesus Christ. In all His manifestation accounts of serenity, my favorite is in Matthew 8:23-27, where He rebukes the storm in the marvelousness of His disciples. You can find the same account in the book of Mark. But let us briefly recall the event. I will paraphrase it: The disciples and Jesus were in the boat, going from point A to

B. Jesus decided to take a nap. The storm hit, but He was sound asleep while the disciples were panicking. With the storm raging, He did not get up. At this point, we can ask boldly: Who the heck can be sound sleep while in a small boat in the middle of a raging storm in the middle of the ocean? Do you know anybody? We are not talking here about a person who is in the middle of the storm, losing all hope of survival, and just gives up to die. We all know at least one of those people. They give up at any small sign of adversity.

Jesus was poised and serene because He knows himself and knows that He has power over all elements. One might argue of Him being God, which is fair. But remember all Jesus' teachings, "greater ye shall do." He has paved the way for us to do the same things He has accomplished and even more. We just must be sound in our faith. "It shall be done unto thee even as you believed."

Calmness and poise are a must if we want to achieve anything great in our life experience and even more to sustain it. It is the outer presence of the person who governs himself. He has become a master of his emotions and thoughts and feelings. This simply means he goes through all of life's unpleasant circumstances like everybody else, but he handles them differently. He does not give power to them by complaining or whining about them to others. He does not fight them, getting involved emotionally because he understands the law of attraction and faith that if he does so, he will get more of those unpleasant situations, which are his beliefs. He focuses instead on the achieved feelings of his desires in that situation, and he overcomes them.

Serenity cuts off all fears, worries, grievances, unworthiness, lacks, envies, jealousies, self-condemnations, any negative emotions. The individual now remains true to his ideals, knowing that he is divinely guided and that all events are there to help him accomplish his desires.

Firm and Exquisite in Manifestation

Notes

Conclusion

Life is an open door for those who know where they are going. Those who have a direction, a destination are more positive and have a positive outlook on events and circumstances that happen to them. They don't let themselves get sidetracked, especially when they understand the power of creation. Understanding the power of creation is first and foremost what you want, your desire. I have never seen anybody create anything without first setting in their mind what they intend to achieve. Even if the result is not what they are expecting (good or bad), the decision to go for some definite purpose led them there. If the outcome is bad, one might consider that as a failure. But there is no such thing as failure going for our desires; it is what I call "Not readiness."

Not readiness is when a person takes action (acts) too soon toward the objective desire without first having mental awareness or mental consciousness of that which is desired. So, he fails on his first attempt, second attempt, or more, but is not a failure until he decides to give up on his desires or dreams. There is always a lesson to be learned from every failed attempt to push us toward our destination.

When the result turns positive and not the outcome we were shooting for, we call it a lucky break or serendipity. That can be the start of one's ascension. But one must search and correct the defects that caused the wrong trajectory in the first place. If not, sooner or later, the shadow of that failure at the doorstep on one's mind will come back even stronger and ruin the nice accomplishments due to his/her unreadiness.

We strongly suggest that everyone take these switches seriously and apply them to their lives for the reasons described above. All of them are important and play a major part for any person who wants to discover their desires and achieve them. Each switch is dimmable, meaning that the individual is not always required to be on top of his game at all times to be successful, but more than seventy percent of application is a must to get the guaranteed result. Just remind yourself of the switches 5 and how you will feel when you achieve that objective.

Look around you. There's abundance ready to be achieved and enjoyed. For those who purposely decide and find their purpose and desire and pay the price of mental toughness by going through these switches, to those, all heavenly and worldly doors will open in perfect divine order.

To those we say, they are FEMming!\
Well, just FEM it!\
Olou-Femy Satty\
Entrepreneur, CEO, President & Author

Conclusion

WWLM, Inc. is a charitable non-profit work supporting those in need throughout the world

Our Programs

- Feeding
- Humanitarian Relief
- Ministry
- LEAP
- Shipping
- TEACH

Become a Lighthouse Keeper through monthly committed giving of $100 or more to any program

Visit www.wwlm.org for all Current Endeavors!

P.O. BOX 5010, MANCHESTER CT 06045 | 860-645-4198

 @WWLMissions  @WWLMissions ✉ wwlm@wwlm.org www.wwlm.org

CPSIA information can be obtained
at www.ICGtesting.com
Printed in the USA
BVHW042010060223
657986BV00004B/36